Water Crisis Survival Guide

Everything You Need to Know to Survive the Coming Water Shortage

Legal Notice:

This eBook is copyright protected. This is only for personal use. You cannot amend, distribute, sell, use, quote or paraphrase any part or the content within this eBook without the consent of the author or copyright owner. Legal action will be pursued if this is breached.

Disclaimer Notice:

Please note the information contained within this document is for educational purposes only.

Every attempt has been made to provide accurate, up to date and reliable complete information no warranties of any kind are expressed or implied. Readers acknowledge that the author is not engaging in rendering legal, financial or professional advice.

By reading any document, the reader agrees that under no circumstances are we responsible for any losses, direct or indirect, which are incurred as a result of use of the information contained within this document, including – but not limited to errors, omissions, or inaccuracies.

TABLE OF CONTENTS

INTRODUCTION 6
    Water: Our Most Important Commodity 6
    How Much Water Do We Need? 7
    Overview of Topics to Be Covered 9
WATER SHORTAGE 11
    NASA Mega Drought Warning 12
    Possible Causes of a Water Shortage 13
    Water Survival Myths 15
THE WORST CASE SCENARIO 17
    What a Large-Scale Water Shortage Would Look Like 17
        Water Rationing 18
        Water on the Black Market 18
        Food Shortages 19
        Societal Breakdown 19
        Mortality Rates 20
        Water Wars 20
WATER SURVIVAL PLAN 21
    Water Storage 22
    Water Procurement Strategies 23
        Rain Barrels 23
        Cisterns 24
        Snow and Ice Melt 25

- Products 25
- Emergency Water Supplies in and around the House 25
- Other Water Sources 26
- WATER HARVESTING DEVICES 29
  - Water from Air Devices 29
  - Water Desalination *Devices* 30
  - Evaporation Solar Stills 31
  - Vegetation Still 32
- WATER TESTING AND PURIFICATION 34
  - The Importance of Testing Water 34
  - Water Testing Methods 35
  - Water Purification Methods 36
    - Filters 36
  - Tablets and Drops 36
  - Charcoal 37
    - Boiling 38
    - Chlorine Dioxide Tablets 38
    - Sunlight 38
    - Distillation 39
    - Reverse Osmosis 39
    - Bleach 40
- GROWING FOOD WITHOUT WATER 41
  - Corn 42
  - Amaranth 42
  - Jerusalem Artichokes 43
  - Sweet Potatoes 43
  - Nopale Cactus 43

Black-eyed Peas 44
Watermelon 44
Other Crops 44
SANITATION WITHOUT WATER 47
Cleaning Clothes 47
Personal Hygiene 49
Disposing of Human Waste without Water 49
    Suburban/Rural Area 50
    Urban Area 51
DO IT YOURSELF 53
Water Filters 53
    Cloth Filter 54
    Multi-layer Filter 54
Atmospheric Water Generator 55
Desalinator 56
Vegetation Still 59
WATER SURVIVAL PLAN AND CHECKLIST 61
Emergency Water Sources 62
Water Testing Supplies 63
Water Purifying Supplies 63
Water Harvesting Supplies and Devices 63
Other items 64
CONCLUSION 66

INTRODUCTION

Many people, when they think about planning for emergencies, focus on laying in a supply of food for their families. They stockpile canned foods and other non-perishables, and food for the family pets. What they don't realize is that a far more likely, and more deadly, crisis would involve a serious shortage of water.

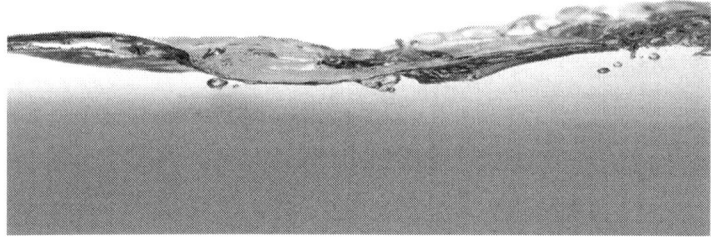

Already, places like California and the Pacific Northwest are experiencing serious droughts. Some estimates say that California will run out of water within a year. The threat of a severe water shortage is one you cannot afford to ignore.

Water: Our Most Important Commodity

How necessary is water? It can be an easy thing to take for granted, but it shouldn't be. Water is the stuff of life. Approximately 71% of the Earth's surface is covered with water. Without it, our planet would not be able to sustain life.

Our bodies are mostly made of water, and every one of our organs and cells needs water to function properly. Water keeps our blood flowing and our hearts pumping, and it keeps our blood pressure under control. It helps to regulate our body temperature; it aids in the digestive process, and it helps keep our bodies clear of toxins.

We are constantly losing water from our bodies, which is why we need to drink water every day. We lose water when we sweat and urinate. We also lose it when we breathe. When it is very warm outside, or when we work hard, we lose more water. Under conditions of extreme stress, we can lose as much as 1.5 liters of water per hour. Consequently, we need to take in more water to replenish our bodies and keep them healthy.

In terms of survival, water is far more important than food. In theory, a person could survive as long as three weeks without food. Mahatma Gandhi survived a 21-day hunger strike. Going without food that long would certainly be unpleasant, but it would not necessarily be fatal. Going without water for that long would be impossible. At most, a person can live a week without water, but that conditions would have to be ideal for that to be possible. In moderate temperatures, if you didn't have to work too much or be exposed to direct sunlight, a week might be possible. However, in real world conditions, surviving three or four days without water would probably be the best you could expect.

How Much Water Do We Need?

If you're like most people, you probably don't have a clear idea of how much water you use in a day. Most of us use far more than we need, but it is equally true that we need more than we think we do. In some parts of the world, clean potable water is hard to find. In the United States, we shower every day. We use vast amounts of water to clean out clothes and dishes and to keep our lawns green. But luxuries like a green lawn aside, how much water do you need per day?

According to the World Health Organization (WHO) the average person needs to drink between 2.5 and 3 liters of water every day. People in cooler climates can get away with drinking less than people who live in hot, dry climates.

That might seem like a lot, but it's merely one part of the picture. Drinking water is important, but refreshment is not the only reason we use water. In addition to drinking water, the average person needs:

- Two to six liters per day for personal hygiene and cleaning
- Three to six liters per day for cooking

These requirements may vary depending upon cultural norms, but they represent a good ballpark figure for understanding how important water is to our survival. On average, each person in your family will need between eight and fifteen liters of water per day, every day. For a family of four, that means you would conceivably need 1,800 liters of water to survive for one month.

That's a lot of water. How prepared are you for a water shortage? Do you know how to find and purify water? Do you have room to store it? The purpose of this book is to give you all of the information you need to shepherd your family through a serious water crisis.

Overview of Topics to Be Covered

A world water crisis isn't a possibility – it's a probability. Most people are not remotely prepared for it, but it is coming. The information in this book is designed to give the tools and information you need to weather the crisis whenever it comes. The first two chapters will lay the groundwork for why water is so important, and why you need to start preparing now. There are a lot of potential things that could prompt a water crisis, and you need to know what they are. We'll talk about drought, water wars, water pollution and contamination, and more. We'll also talk a look at what a worst case scenario would look like, so you understand the urgency of the situation.

The rest of the book will be dedicated to giving you practical advice on how to prepare for a water crisis. In the second chapter, we'll go over how to make a basic water crisis survival plan. It's important to know where and how to find water, and to have the information you need to find it. A big part of survival is doing whatever you can to give yourself an advantage, and mapping out your area and understanding the resources that are available to you is a big part of that.

The third and fourth chapters have to do with harvesting, testing, and purifying water. We'll review the different kinds of water harvesting devices that are available, and go through the different ways you can test the safety of your water supply and purify water as needed.

The fifth and sixth chapters will talk about ways to minimize the amount of water you use on a daily basis. In a crisis, it's important to use the smallest amount of water possible for purposes other than drinking, so you can be sure that you have enough to drink. We'll talk about ways to keep your home sanitary without using water. We'll also go over ways to grow food without water. Without adequate water, the food supply will dwindle too. The people who understand how to grow food without using a lot of water will have a real advantage over the people who don't.

The seventh chapter will give you instructions on how to build your own water purification devices. If you have the money to buy purifiers now and would rather do that, the book includes recommendations of water purifiers to consider. However, in a serious drought or other water crisis, it will probably be difficult to buy a purifier. There will be widespread panic, and any available purification devices will sell out quickly. Because of that, it's important to know how to build your own purifier. Some of the available devices cost thousands of dollars, but you can build a purifier for considerably less than that.

The final chapter will consist of a handy water survival plan and checklist so you can have an easy way to make sure you have everything you need. The checklists will include items for water storage, water testing, water purification, construction, waste management, personal hygiene, drought gardening, groceries, and other essential items.

The water crisis is coming. Our water supplies are dwindling every day, and the time will come when your survival will depend on being able to find, gather, and purify the water you need. Not every family will survive it, but your family will if you follow the advice in this book.

WATER SHORTAGE

How probable is a serious water crisis? Do you really need to be worried about having enough water? How important is it to prepare?

The world is headed for a serious water shortage. There is no point in pretending that's not the case. Our planet is getting drier and drier, and the population is growing. Our supply of water is not endless. Parts of the country that are normally lush and green are dry. California is in a water emergency, and even parts of the country that we think of as rainy, like the Pacific Northwest, are dangerously dry.

NASA Mega Drought Warning

Let's start by talking about the risk of drought. NASA has been scanning images of the Earth to evaluate the severity of the water shortage, and the information they have released is alarming.

Much of the West Coast is already in serious trouble. Not only is surface water drying up, but subterranean water sources are in trouble, too.

One of the things that concerns NASA is the rate of greenhouse gas emissions. At the current rate, or even if our emission rates drop a bit, a good portion of the United States will experience catastrophic drought in this century. For many of us, the historical benchmark for serious drought is the Dust Bowl of the 1930s. That was a serious drought that lasted ten years and caused "black blizzards" of dust that covered landscapes and buildings with dirt.

The drought that NASA predicts could make the Dust Bowl look like a walk in the park. Their current estimates are that we are going to face a mega drought that could last thirty or forty years. The western and southwestern states are likely to be the hardest hit, but a serious water shortage there will affect the entire world. California grows a huge amount of the food we eat, and without water, food production will come to a halt. If NASA's projections are correct, we could be looking at the kind of drought that only happens once a millennium.

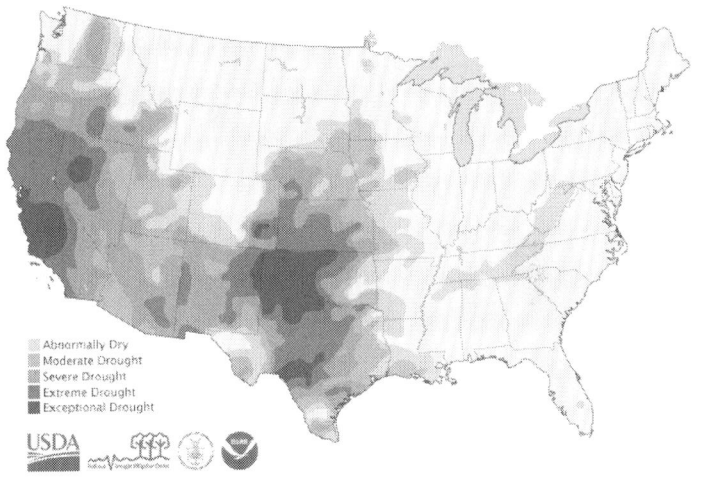

Possible Causes of a Water Shortage

A mega drought is only one of the things we need to be concerned about when it comes to the state of our water supply. There are other crises looming that could precipitate a major shortage, some natural and some man-made.

- Dwindling water supplies are a problem all around the world. NASA's analysis of groundwater levels is alarming. The level of water in every major aquifer around the world is on a steady decline, and there's no end in sight. Typically,

- groundwater is only used in emergencies. Due to rainfall shortages we are dipping into those emergency stores more frequently, and we have no way to replenish them.
- Water shortages played a role in the recent civil war in Syria, and if the current trends continue, water could be a source of civil unrest everywhere. In the past, countries have gone to war over land and ideologies, but many experts feel that water will be the resource we fight over in the future. Already, one-fifth of the world's population is living in places where there is not enough water to support them. Given how essential water is to human survival, it is only a matter of time until people in drought-stricken countries start venturing over borders in an effort to get what they need.
- The amount of water available is the first order of concern, but it's not the only one. What would happen if our remaining supplies of water were contaminated? Water contamination is a very real possibility, and there are a few things that could cause it. For example, microorganisms like E. coli and Legionella (the bacterium that causes Legionnaire's disease) could get into the water supply. Man-made contaminants such as disinfectants and industrial chemicals could leach into the water supply from surrounding areas. Radiation is another potential source of contamination – natural and man-made deposits of radioactive material could deteriorate and make their way into the water supply.
- Water-borne illness is a big potential problem. As water supplies grow scarce, people may be inclined to use unsanitary water for drinking. They may also wash less, which can encourage the spread of fecal matter and the diseases that travel with it. Some of the diseases that could become epidemics in the event of a severe drought include cholera, typhoid, amoebic dysentery, Lassa virus, and hookworm.

Water-borne illnesses already kill about 4,000 children per day worldwide. In the event of a serious shortage, those numbers would increase exponentially. In the United States, good sanitation and our ample (for now) supply of water means that things like diarrhea are not deadly. However, in developing areas of the world where water is already scarce, that is not the case. Diarrhea and dysentery can be deadly in the absence of good hygiene and sanitation. Both diseases cause the people who have them to become dehydrated, too, which means that they pose an even greater risk than they would under normal circumstances.

Water Survival Myths

One of the most disturbing things about the coming water crisis is how much misinformation people have about water. Some of the information we carry around in our heads is based on arbitrary things while some is simply outdated or incorrect. Let's look at some of the most common water survival myths:

- You need eight eight-ounce glasses of water per day. This particular myth has proven to be a very enduring one. It came from the Food and Nutrition Board in 1945, and it's been going strong ever since. The thing that makes this myth dangerous is that the amount of water you need can vary depending on where you live, how old you are, and how much physical labor you'll be doing. There's no fixed amount. Your body needs what it needs, and it may be more or less than the sixty-four ounces you've heard about.
- The second myth is just as dangerous. It has to do with finding drinkable water around your house in a crisis. If the water supply is contaminated or otherwise compromised, you may get a warning from your municipality to turn off your water. Some of the water you find around your house is potable. For example, you can use water from melted ice cubes or your water heater. However, the water in radiators

may contain lead, the water in water beds may contain bacteria and fungi, and the same goes for the water in your toilet bowl. (The water in the tank behind the toilet is safe to use.)
- The third myth has to do with bottled water. Many people think of bottled water as being safer than tap water, but that is simply not the case. In fact, the Food and Drug Administration (FDA) has issued over one hundred recalls of bottled water in recent years. Some of the reasons for the recalls include finding of mold, kerosene, glass, fecal matter, algae, and yeast. One study at Syracuse University showed that bottled water had 1,000% more bacteria than tap water.
- The fourth myth is about drinking running water. While running water, such as the water in streams and brooks, is a better choice than stagnant water, the fact that it is running does not mean you shouldn't purify it. Running water can still contain bacteria and other contaminants. To be safe, you should always purify any water you find.
- The fifth myth has to do with drinking salt water. You may have heard that it is safe to drink small amounts of salt water in an emergency, but that is not true. Drinking salt water will actually speed the rate at which you become dehydrated. You can use it to cool your body if it's warm outside, but never drink it.
- Finally, the sixth myth has to do with eating snow. It is true that snow is frozen water, but there are a couple of reasons why eating snow is not the best way to hydrate your body. The first is that snow that's been sitting on the ground may be contaminated with bacteria, fungus, and chemicals. The second is that eating snow can wreak havoc with your body's temperature. Your body has to work hard to heat the snow, and that means it uses more water. If you do use snow, it should be fresh-fallen, and you should melt it first and then drink it.

A serious water shortage is an inevitability. It is not possible to know which factor – drought, contamination, or water wars – will be the thing that sends the world into a water crisis, but the specific cause matters less than what will follow. In the next chapter, we'll take a look at what a severe water crisis would mean.

THE WORST CASE SCENARIO

Water is already running low, and in California, Ohio, and Detroit, citizens have lost access to supplies of clean water. The western United States is in the middle of an unprecedented drought that threatens the entire country. Things are scary, and they're only going to get worse. To understand how important, it is to prepare your family to survive a water crisis, let's look at a worst case scenario situation.

What a Large-Scale Water Shortage Would Look Like

What would a severe water shortage look like in the United States? If you live in a part of the country that hasn't yet been hit by a serious drought like the one in the western states, you might have a hard time imagining it. To get an idea of what it would be like, let's look at a real-world example.

The city of New Delhi faced a serious water crisis at the end of 2014. Their shortage was due to governmental mismanagement of water supplies, not drought, but the results would be the same regardless of the cause. Approximately 40% of the people who live in New Delhi did not have access to the municipal water supply. Every day, water supply trucks would drive the streets, stopping for a few minutes to let citizens claim a few liters of water. There was never enough to go around, and it was not uncommon for people to fight over the little water that was available.

It would be a mistake to dismiss the example of New Delhi for any reason. Here are some of the things we can expect if a serious water crisis hits the United States.

Water Rationing

Water rationing will become the norm. Citizens in California and other western states are already experiencing it, but the government will have to take decisive action to conserve the water that is available. In World War II, people in London were only allowed to fill their bathtubs with a few inches of water to clean themselves.

Today, we might see the government turn off water supplies for most of the day to limit use. Water usage would be strictly limited. The primary concerns would be drinking water and  municipal sanitation, and everything else would be secondary. That means you would not be able to use the public water supply for watering your garden, or even for taking showers.

Water on the Black Market

Criminals would tap into the water supply, and a black market for water would spring up. If you think that this sounds too alarmist to be plausible, keep in mind that it already happened in New Delhi.

Criminals in Lemoore, California, have already tapped into four fire hydrants to steal water, and there is no reason to expect that behavior will stop. There will always be a percentage of people who will look to profit in a crisis. If municipalities are unable to protect the water supply, many citizens will be forced to turn to the black market to get what they need.

Food Shortages

People all across the United States are dependent upon crops grown here for their survival. If we experienced a serious water shortage, a food shortage would be inevitable. Crops in California and other western states are already in danger of dying.

If the water crisis continues to worsen, there will not be enough to grow crops. Food supplies will run short, and people will be desperate. Food will turn up on the black market too, and there will be a risk of rioting and civil unrest as people try to get what they need.

Societal Breakdown

As the crisis escalates, civilized behavior will become a thing of the past. Even the most morally upstanding people will stoop to acts of thievery and violence if their lives depend on it. In the event of a catastrophic crisis of both food and water, it would be very difficult for police to maintain control of the nation's cities. Governors will call out the National Guard, and we will be in a state of martial law. Even with the military on the streets, citizens will have to protect themselves. Anyone who is not prepared to take up arms against people on the hunt for food and water will be at risk of serious injury or even death.

Mortality Rates

In a serious water shortage, it would not take long for people to start getting sick. Sanitation will be difficult with limited water, and the water supplies will quickly become contaminated with fecal matter, bacteria, viruses, algae, chemicals, and other contaminants. People who drink the water without purifying it properly will get sick. Diseases like cholera and dysentery will spread rapidly, and, lacking the water to properly sanitize or disinfect our belongings, we will be unable to stop them from turning into pandemics. Hospitals will be overloaded with patients, and the healthcare system will be completely overwhelmed and unable to respond. Young children and the elderly will be especially vulnerable at first, but eventually even the strongest and healthiest people would be at risk.

Water Wars

Already, there is a crisis brewing between the United States and Mexico about the water in the Rio Grande. The governments of the two countries have a water utilization treaty that has been in place since 1945. Texas is experiencing a very serious drought, and at present, the Mexican government owes the United States approximately 380,000 acre-feet of water, which would be enough to take care of 1.5 million Texans for a year. It is not difficult to imagine a scenario in which the United States would be forced to go after Mexican water supplies in an effort to save lives.

The risk of a serious water crisis is real, and it is not something you can afford to ignore. The problem is already serious, and we lack any real capacity to take action to rectify it. We can't force it to rain in California, and we have no way to replenish our dwindling groundwater supplies. Most people do not understand how serious the crisis is, and they are using more water than they need to right now.

The people who will be best prepared to survive a water crisis are the people who take the time to prepare now. Once the crisis hits and the municipal water supply in your area is unavailable, it will be too late for you to do much to protect your family. You need to have a plan in place, and you need to have the tools and supplies you need to survive.

The first step is having a water survival plan, and that is what we will talk about in the next chapter.

WATER SURVIVAL PLAN

If you don't already have a water survival plan, now is the time to make one. The majority of people are not going to be prepared, and you don't want to be like them. To start with, you need to know how you can safely store water, and how much to store.

Water Storage

Let's start with the basics of water storage. The general rule of thumb is to store about 2.5 liters (or one gallon) of potable water for every person and pet in your household. You would need additional water for hygiene and other uses, but non-potable water is easier to come by, and it's not as urgent to store it. You can do it if you have the room, but for now, let's talk about potable water. You should plan on storing enough potable water for at least two weeks – more if you have room. Here's a simple storage method you can use.

- Collect plastic waters and jugs. You can use empty juice containers, soda bottles, and water bottles. Do not use milk containers. Milk is hard to remove and if any remains in the bottle it will contaminate the water.
- Clean each container thoroughly with dishwashing soap and water, and rinse them so that no soap remains inside of the bottles.
- Rinse each bottle with a solution of one teaspoon of unscented chlorine bleach and one quart of water. Shake the bottles so that the bleach touches every surface, and then empty the solution out and rinse the bottles again. Make sure to sanitize the lids and caps as well.
- Put on gloves and refill the bottles with fresh tap water.

Add two drops of unscented chlorine bleach to each bottle, and reseal it tightly with the original lid.

Take a Sharpie and date each bottle, and store it in a cool, dry place.

As a rule, you should plan on rotating out your water every six months or so. Even if you sanitize the bottles, there is still a risk that bacteria or other agents could get into the bottles and contaminate them. If you have the storage space, you can relabel the older water as non-potable, and save it for washing or other purposes.

Another option is to buy 55-gallon water storage barrels, which come complete with siphons and instructions on how to use them. You can purchase and store bottled water. If there is any question about the safety of the water, you can purify it – something we'll talk more about later.

Water Procurement Strategies

The next step of your water survival plan is to have the equipment you need to procure more water. Let's talk about some options, and then I will provide you with links to some specific products that you may want to consider.

Rain Barrels

One option you can use to collect water is a rain barrel system. Rain barrels collect the water that runs off your roof when it rains. If you want to use rain barrels, you need to make sure that your roof does not have any toxic materials. Things to avoid include asbestos, tar, gravel, and treated cedar shakes. You should also test your gutter to make sure they don't contain lead. A good rain barrel will have a screen to keep out insects and a tight-fitting lid. You should also make sure that there is a safe place for overflow water to go. It is best to put the barrels in a place where the overflow will run downhill and not into the foundation of your house.

If you decide to use rain barrels, make sure to check your local state requirements. Many states have regulations regarding how you can collect rainwater, and you may need to get a permit. You should also check to see if there are tax benefits to using rainwater. Texas residents get a tax break for using rain barrels, and other states may as well.

The other thing to keep in mind if you decide to collect rainwater is that you will need to filter and treat it if you want to drink it. Actually, you'll want to filter it even if you use it for hygiene only, to make sure you get any dirt or leaves that end up in your barrels. A lot of people who collect rainwater use the water for cleaning and hygiene and rely on other sources for drinking water.

Cisterns

If you have the space and the budget for it, installing a cistern is a big step up from rain barrels and can allow you to store enough water for an end-of-the-world type situation. A cistern is basically a giant water tank that stores rainwater. They can hold between 1,400 and 12,000 gallons of water. The tanks are plastic, but they are usually not food-grade, so if you plan on drinking the water from your cistern you will need to treat it first. You can use it for cleaning and hygiene without treating it, just like you can water from rain barrels.

Installing a cistern is a big step, and it's not inexpensive. It's also not portable, so you'll want to make sure to have smaller containers you can take with you if you need to bug out. Many preppers store water in a variety of ways. For example, you buy bottled water or have jugs that hold five to seven gallons of water each. Those are small enough that you can take them with you if you need to.

Snow and Ice Melt

Another option is to collect snow and ice and melt it. When it snows, you can use a clean tarp to collect the snow as it falls. Typically, snow that has just fallen can be used as drinking water without being treated, but if you have doubts or live in an area with heavy air pollution, you should purify it first. It is better to add chemicals when the melted snow or ice has warmed up a bit, as they will be more effective then. Ice tends to yield more water than snow. You can pour water collected from ice and snow through a coffee filter to remove any debris, and then purify it as you would any other water.

Products

Before we move on to talking about other sources of water in and around your house, here are a few products to consider:

Emergency Water Storage System (100 Gallons)

Water Storage Kit (55 Gallons)

Water Storage Tank (250 Gallons)

Water Preserve Concentrate (Enough to treat 55 gallons of water)

Buying a storage system can make it easier to purify and store the water your family needs.

Emergency Water Supplies in and around the House

In the event of a water crisis, there are some places inside your home where you can find potable water:

- Inside your hot water tank. You can drain the water and purify it.
- Inside fire hydrants. If you have a fire hydrant nearby, you can tap it and use the water as needed.
- Inside your toilet tanks. It is important to note that the water inside the tank (in the back of the toilet) can be used, not the water in the bowl.
- Liquids in canned foods. Storing canned foods makes sense because they are non-perishable, and they contain water, so you are getting extra water storage as well as food.
- Swimming pool or hot tub. If you have a pool, you can use the water in it in an emergency.
- Gutters. Any water that has collected in your gutters can be purified and used. Make sure your gutters are free of lead and other contaminants.
- Water pipes. Even if your municipal water supply is turned off, you will have water trapped in your pipes that is drinkable.
- Ice cubes in the freezer. If you have ice cubes in your freezer, you can melt them and drink the water. In the event that a water crisis coincides with a power outage, make sure to take the bagged ice cubes out of the freezer and put them in a container where they can melt.

Other Water Sources

Just as you need to know where to find usable water in your house, it is also important to know where you can find water nearby. If you live in a very dry climate there may not be many local sources of natural water, but if a water shortage is caused by contamination or some other problem (as opposed to a drought) you may be able to use local bodies of water as a source.

One good way to scope out water sources in your area is to use Google Maps. All you need to do is type in the name of your municipality with the word "map" after it, and you will get a local map that shows bodies of water. Not all of them will be labeled – Google is still working on that – but you'll be able to see where they are. The nice thing about Google Maps is that it will show you natural bodies of water as well as things like water traps on golf courses. Here's a map of part of Washington State, so you know what to expect:

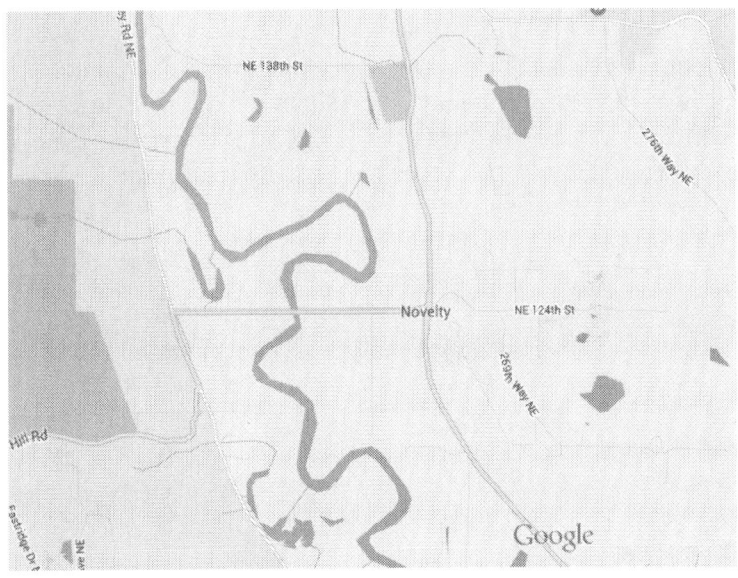

As you can see, there is a large river on the map, as well as several smaller water sources. Zooming in will give you names for some bodies of water, but even if there isn't a name, you'll be able to map out how to get there using the other information available – street names, landmarks, and so on.

The best way to prepare for getting water from these sources is to print out maps of your municipality and surrounding towns and cities now and keep them on hand. The possibility exists that a water shortage will happen simultaneously with another big problem, such as a storm, a deliberate attack by terrorists, or a pandemic. If that's the case, you may not have access to the internet. For example, if terrorists or a hostile nation launched an EMP attack against the United States, it would knock out all of the electronics in the affected areas. You should also print maps of the area around your bug out location if you have one.

You may want to consider doing a more detailed scoping out of your area by printing maps and then surveilling the bodies of water you find. It can also be helpful to make note of swimming pools and fountains in your area. Water taken from public places will need to be treated before you can drink it, but the thing to remember is that people are going to be panicking if they lose access to water. If you know all of the places you can find water, you will be in a far better position to protect your family than the people who don't.

Here are some of the places you may be able to find water in your area:

- Rivers
- Lakes
- Ponds
- Streams
- Reservoirs
- Creeks
- Natural Springs
- Swimming pools
- Water traps on golf courses
- Fountains

The more comprehensive your list is, the better able you will be to find the water you need for your family.

WATER HARVESTING DEVICES

Because the threat of a worldwide water shortage is so serious, some companies are working to come up with new ways to harvest drinkable water. This chapter will look at some of the innovations that are out there. There will be a brief description of what each device is and how it works, as well as links to some specific products you may want to consider.

Later in the book, there will be specific instructions on how you can construct watering devices of your own. Many of the devices listed in this chapter are expensive. If you have the money to buy them, that's great – but you don't need to spend a lot to construct them.

Water from Air Devices

One of the most promising technologies out there comes from an Israeli company called Water-Gen. The idea of harvesting water from the air isn't new, but they've found a way to make it cost-effective and deliver high-quality purified water. Their system uses the same general principle as air conditioning. When the air enters the unit, it is chilled and dehumidified, which extracts the water from the air. The water is then filtered, purified, and stored in an internal tank where it is preserved to maintain its quality.

At present, the system the offer can collect between 65 and 210 gallons of drinkable water per day. Atmospheric water collection will work as long as certain conditions are met:

- The ambient temperature must be at least 35 degrees Fahrenheit.
- The percentage of humidity must be above 40%.
- The elevation must be less than 4,000 feet.

At present, the atmospheric water collector made by Water-Gen being used by the military, but they say that civilian applications are inevitable. In the meantime, here are a couple of other products to consider:

Aquaboy Atmospheric Water Generator (stores 35 gallons)

Aquaboy Atmospheric Water Generator (stores 3.5 gallons)

These options are both pricey, but later in the book I'll tell you how to make your own atmospheric water generator for about three hundred dollars.

Water Desalination *Devices*

Another option for people who live near the ocean is to get or make a water desalination device. As you know, salt water is not drinkable – in fact, drinking it will make you get dehydrated more quickly than not drinking water at all. Desalination devices work by removing the salt from ocean water so you can drink it.

One of the biggest drawbacks to desalinating water is that it requires a lot of energy to do it. The water must be heated. If you only need to collect water for a few people, here's a simple way you can do it at home:

1. Place a heavy metal cup in a large pan.
2. Pour salt water into the pan, making sure it does not get into the cup.
3. Place the lid of the pan upside down on top of the pan, so the center of it is over the cup.
4. Bring the water to a gentle boil (a hard boil will throw salt into the cup, so it's important not to have the heat too high.)
5. As the water boils, it will steam. The steam will collect on the lid and drip into the cup, and the salt and other minerals in the water will stay in the pan.

Here are a couple of products to consider if you want to be able to desalinate larger amounts of water:

SeaPack Water Filter (takes sea water, desalinates it, and adds electrolytes to make a sports drink)

Katadyn Survivor 35 Desalinator (produces 4.5 liters per hour, used by the military)

Later in the book, I'll tell you how to make a water desalinator of your own.

Evaporation Solar Stills

Solar stills represent another way to collect moisture from the air and the soil. They use the heat of the sun to distill the water, so they are more energy efficient than devices that require electricity. There are two basic types. A pit still consists of a hole in the ground covered with a sheet of plastic. When the sun hits the plastic, it acts as a greenhouse and condenses the water from the surrounding soil, which runs down and collects into the cup. A box still is a little more complex – it uses the heat of the sun to distill water that is poured into it, and it will work as a desalination device as well.

Here's one product to consider:

Aquamate Solar Still (collects 0.5 to 2.0 liters per day, usable at sea and on land)

Later in the book, I'll tell you how to make your own solar still.

Vegetation Still

The final type of still we'll discuss in this chapter is a vegetation still. Vegetation stills can be used to collect water from plants. Any edible plant contains some water – plants like succulents hold more water than regular leaves, but any vegetation will do. The most important thing to remember if you decide to gather water from vegetation is not to use any poisonous plants because the toxins will end up in the resulting water.

You can make a very simple makeshift vegetation still using a plastic bag. All you need to do is to collect enough vegetation to mostly fill the bag. You will need to mash the leaves to break down the leaves' water-resistant outer layer. Seal the bag and leave it in the sun. The heat from the sun will cause a greenhouse effect inside the bag. The water inside of the plants will condense and run down into the bottom of the bag.

The resulting water will have a very strong leafy flavor, but it will be potable. You can also add vegetation to a regular evaporation still to extract the water from it, but you'll have to clean out the leaves afterward. It's best to do this at night when the still is less effective.

It's important to note that you will still need to purify the water after you collect it. In a water emergency, you won't want to waste water washing the plants first. Instead, you can collect the water and then boil it or purify it with bleach or tablets.

Here is one product to consider:

Vegetation Solar Still Kit (includes collection and storage bags, as well as water purification tablets)

The benefit of having one or more ways to collect water from unexpected sources like the air, soil, or plants is that it will give you a leg up on people who are less prepared. The collection techniques mentioned here are all viable ways to get drinkable water for your family. When water is scarce, the competition for what's available is going to be fierce. While other people are fighting over bottled water, you can stay home and collect water from your environment.

Collecting water is important, but it is equally vital to know how to take the water you have collected and make it safe to drink. There are a number of different methods you can use, and we'll talk about all of them in the next chapter.

WATER TESTING AND PURIFICATION

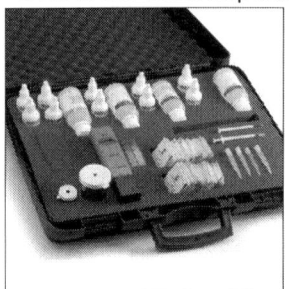

One of the most important things you need to know how to do in the event of a serious water crisis is differentiate between potable and non-potable water. Testing water before you drink it is essential. Many people won't know what to do, and will end up drinking unsafe water. Knowing how to test and purify water is going to be one of the things that determines who survives, and who doesn't.

The Importance of Testing Water

Drinking contaminated water can have very serious effects on you and your family. Unsafe drinking water may contain:

- Bacteria
- Viruses
- Algae
- Chemicals
- Salt
- Toxins

Regardless of where you find or collect water, the best approach is to purify it if you have any doubts at all about its safety. Purifying water that is already safe to drink is not going to hurt anything, and water safety is not something you want to mess around with. This chapter will walk you through the various methods you can use to test and purify your water.

Water Testing Methods

The first thing you can do to test water is to use your senses. If you find or collect water, here are some things to look for:

- A pond that has murky water and bugs living in it is a better choice than a crystal-clear pond. That might seem counterintuitive, but water with living things in it is probably well oxygenated and has a healthy pH balance. Crystal clear water might be laden with chemicals.
- Some microorganisms are visible to the naked eye. If you look at water and see tiny parasites in it, don't drink it.

Smell the water. Water with a strong smell of chemicals, or a metallic smell, is probably not safe to drink. Some metals are fine, but drinking water with high levels of lead or mercury is not safe. Water with a strong smell of organic matter might taste funny, but it's probably safe to drink if you purify it first.

-

The only sure-fire way to know if water is safe to drink is to buy a testing kit. Here are a couple of good options:

First Alert Drinking Water Test Kit

PurTest Home Water Analysis Testing Kit

It's probably a good idea to buy a kit and keep it in your house or in your bug-out bag.

Water Purification Methods

As stated earlier, the safest thing to do is to purify any water you are planning to drink if you are not 100% sure that it is safe. Here are some water purification methods you can use.

Filters

Water filters are widely available, and can be used to remove many harmful things from the water you find, including metals, protozoa, and bacteria. There are portable options available, as well as larger models. These filters generally use charcoal or other methods to remove contaminants from water. It's important to note that while a coffee filter can be used to remove leaves, insects, and large particles, running water through a paper filter will not make it safe to drink. Here are a few commercial filters to consider:

LifeStraw

PerfectWater Purifier

SurvivalStill Emergency Water Purifier

Tablets and Drops

One of the easiest and least expensive ways to purify water is to use commercial tablets or drops. For example, these tablets contain iodine, and one bottle (which costs less than ten dollars) will treat fifty liters of water:

Potable Aqua Water Treatment Tablets

Charcoal

Using charcoal is one of the oldest ways to purify water, and also one of the easiest. Activated charcoal is extremely porous – in fact, one pound of charcoal has a surface area of 100 acres. The many pores and openings in the charcoal trap the impurities in the water, and the water that passes out the other end of the filter is safe to drink.

You can certainly buy filters that use activated charcoal to clean your water, but it's also very easy to make a simple filter at home. Here's what you need to do:

1. Start with fresh charcoal that has cooled completely. You can get fresh charcoal by building a campfire and banking it with dirt or ash once you have a good coal bed in place. A couple of days later, uncover it, and let the charcoal cool.
2. Use a rock or hammer to break the charcoal up into small bits (they should range from being the size of aquarium gravel down to dust.)
3. Find a clean container with one large end and one small end (a good choice is an empty 2-liter soda bottle with the large end sawed off.)
4. Poke a hole in the cap and stuff the neck of the bottle with grass or a piece of fabric. Put the lid back on.
5. Pack the crushed charcoal tightly into the bottle. The water should trickle through, not flow through. If it flows, you need to pack it tighter. Fill the bottle about halfway with charcoal.
6. Place your filter upside down over a container, preferably the same one you will use to boil your water.
7. Pour the water on top of the charcoal and allow it to drip through. You will probably have to filter it two or three times to get it to be clear.

8. Boil the water to remove pathogens and make it safe for drinking.

Boiling

Boiling is the best and easiest way to kill pathogens and other biological matter from water and make it safe to drink. The Wilderness Medical Society says that heating water to 160 degrees Fahrenheit will kill all pathogens within 30 minutes, and heating to 185 degrees will kill them within just a few minutes. Water boils at 212 degrees Fahrenheit, so boiling will kill everything. If you are at a higher altitude, make sure to let the water boil for a minute or so since water boils at a slightly lower temperature at high altitudes.

Chlorine Dioxide Tablets

Chlorine dioxide tablets are an easy, inexpensive, and very portable way to purify water. One tablet will purify one quart of water, and it will protect you against bacteria, viruses, and cysts.

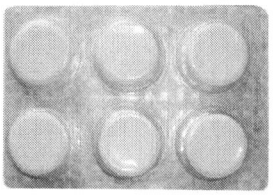

You can buy them online here.

Sunlight

Another very easy (and free) water purification method to use is sunlight. The ultraviolet rays of the sun will kill bacteria and parasites after approximately six hours of exposure to the sun. Here are basic instructions:

1. Filter cloudy or dirty water through a piece of fabric first.

2. Put the water in a clear plastic bottle such as a 2-liter soda bottle.
3. Lay the bottle on its side in direct sunlight. If you put the bottles on a reflective surface, it will speed the process, but laying them on the ground is fine. Try to put them at an angle where the sunlight falls directly on them.
4. As long as the sky is mostly sunny or only partly cloudy, the water will be free of pathogens after six hours. In cloudy weather, it will take two days.

It's important to note that UV rays from the sun will kill bacteria, viruses, and parasites. However, it will not clear water of chemicals or other man-made toxins. Do not use this method if you suspect that the water has chemicals in it.

Distillation

The previous chapter already mentioned various kinds of stills, and you'll get instructions on how to make them later. Distilling water involves boiling it and collecting the steam. Impurities in the water are left behind in the pan or kettle, and the steam condenses leaving only pure water behind.

Reverse Osmosis

Reverse osmosis is the scientific name for one process that can be used to desalinate sea water. Basically, it works by putting a semi-porous membrane made of Gore-Tex in the middle. One side of the tube filled with pure water, and the other with water containing a solute (such as salt.) Osmosis would result in the pure water passing through the membrane and diluting the water on the other side. In reverse osmosis, pressure is applied to the impure water, causing it to pass through the membrane and leave the solute (salt) behind.

Bleach

Using household bleach to purify water is easy and inexpensive. You only need two drops of bleach to purify one quart (or one liter) of water, so a bottle of bleach will last you a long time. Bleach will not get rid of sediment or visible dirt, so if your water is dirty or cloudy, filter it first. You can use almost any kind of clean fabric or fiber as a filtration device. Examples include clean socks, bandanas, feminine hygiene products, or even grass. Filter the water as many times as you need to for it to be clear.

Once your water is clear, put it in a container and add the bleach. It can be difficult to measure two drops. You can either use an eye-dropper or make a simple wick by pouring a little bleach into the cap and putting a small strip of paper towel or toilet paper into the bleach. Let the end of the wick hang over the edge of the cap. The paper will absorb the bleach, and it will drip from the other end, making it easy for you to measure two drops. After you add the bleach, wait 30 minutes before drinking the water. You should also make sure to swish a little of the purified water into the cap of your water bottle. If you don't, the water collected in the threads of the bottle cap could contaminate the water.

You can also use iodine as a way of purifying your water, but it is less ideal than bleach and should be used sparingly. If you get iodine drops, use two drops per quart or liter of water (if the water is clear) and ten drops if the water is cloudy. The iodine will make your water taste a little funny, and it will also turn it slightly orange. You can buy iodine crystals although they are hard to come by, or iodine tablets. The thing to remember about iodine is that it can be toxic in large amounts. You need some to survive, but drinking too much can be harmful. It's also important to note that iodine will kill biological agents, but it will not remove metals or chemicals from your water.

As you can see, there are many different ways to purify water you find and make it safe to drink. Some are more involved than others. It's a good idea to have a combination of large and portable options. For example, you might want to buy or build a large solar still for your home so you can distill large amounts of water at once. At the same time, it makes sense to have a supply of chlorine dioxide tablets, iodine drops, and small plastic bottles. That way if civil unrest or war breaks out and you need to bug out, you will have supplies to bring with you. The simplest method of purifying water is boiling, so as long as you have a pot and a way of starting a fire, you will be able to purify what you need.

GROWING FOOD WITHOUT WATER

In the event of a long-term drought or water emergency, supplies of fresh food would begin to dwindle. Even if you have an ample supply of non-perishable food on hand, eventually you will need to find or grow food to keep your family going.

You already known you can collect rainwater and use it to water crops, but what if the mega drought NASA has warned us about happens, and there isn't any rain? Would you know what things to plant to feed your family?

The good news is that there are several nutritious crops you can grow that require little or no water to thrive. Let's talk about what they are, and what you will need in order to grow them.

Corn

Corn is a staple of the American diet and a great thing to grow because it is so versatile. You can eat it fresh, preserve it, or dry it and grind it into corn meal to use for baking. It's naturally sweet and packed with nutrients, including potassium, magnesium, iron, and Vitamin B-6. Biblical stories about corn suggest that corn is a high-maintenance crop, one that requires a lot of water to grow. Actually, the opposite is true. Corn does very well in low-water environments, which is why it was such a staple of the Aztec diet. Corn does need some water, but on the whole, it's a good choice for a drought situation. Heirloom species, which were around before the days of modern irrigation, tend to be more resilient than modern species are.

Amaranth

Amaranth is popularly referred to as an ancient grain, but it is actually a pseudo cereal like quinoa. What makes it a good choice is that you can eat the leaves as well as the grains, and it will grow without you having to water it much – if it all. It will also reseed itself and come back without you having to replant it, which makes it an easy choice.

The grains require little preparation – all you need to do is put it in water and cook it the way you would rice. Use a ratio of three parts water to one part amaranth. The leaves are easy to prepare, too. Young leaves can be eaten raw while the mature leaves should be cooked slightly. Amaranth is a good source of protein, fiber, calcium, iron, and magnesium.

Jerusalem Artichokes

Jerusalem artichokes are not actually artichokes. Rather, they are tubers like potatoes or yams. They are also called sun chokes. They will grow even if you don't water then, they're perennial, and they generally produce an abundant crop. Because they are tubers, you can prepare them using any method you would use to cook a potato. Baking, roasting, sautéing, pan frying, and boiling all work. They also keep well as long as you store them in a cool, dry place, the same way you would store potatoes or any other tuber.

Jerusalem artichokes are a good source of carbohydrates and fiber, and they also contain magnesium, potassium, and Vitamin B-6.

Sweet Potatoes

Speaking of tubers, sweet potatoes are another good low-water crop to consider. Their lush green leaves shade the soil, which helps to prevent the evaporation of water. In a very long drought, the plants would probably not yield much, but in years with some rain they would do very well. You probably already know that sweet potatoes can be baked, fried, roasted or boiled. They also keep well, making them a good choice to store for winter months when you might not be able to grow much. Sweet potatoes are packed with fiber, Vitamin A, Vitamin C, magnesium, and potassium.

Nopale Cactus

If you're like most people, the first thing you think of when you think about low-water plants are cacti. There are many different species of cactus, and none of them needs water to thrive. The Nopale cactus is a variety of prickly pear that is bred for its tasty pads, or leaves. They have a somewhat slimy texture (similar to okra) but they need almost no water to survive, and you could live on them if you needed to. Nopale cactus is a good source of calcium, manganese, magnesium, fiber, and Vitamins A, B-6, and C.

Black-eyed Peas

Black-eyed peas (also known as cow peas, southern peas, and zipper peas) are a staple of Southern cuisine, and they grow without any artificial irrigation. They can eaten fresh, but then can also be dried and stored, making them a good choice for long-term survival. It is important to keep in mind that if you dry them, you will need water to cook them. In a severe drought, it may make sense to eat them fresh. They're a great source of dietary fiber, potassium, and magnesium. They are also a good choice because they help put nitrogen back into depleted soil, so even though they don't tend to yield a huge crop, it can be beneficial to plant them because it will make it easier for you to grow other things the following year.

Watermelon

It might surprise you to see watermelon on this list, but for a plant named after water, they actually require very little of it to grow. In fact, they're grown in Florida and planted during the least rainy time of the year, and they do remarkably well. Watermelon is delicious, and it can also help keep your family hydrated, which makes it a great drought crop. Watermelon is a terrific source of Vitamins A and C.

Other Crops

The crops above are some of the ones that do best in low-water situations, but there are others to consider. In general, plants with very shallow root systems – such as lettuce – don't do well without water. However, plants with deep roots like tomatoes, squash and melons can do very well because they can pull water from deep within the soil. One species of zucchini, the Dark Star, has been specially bred to do well without water.

Other good choices include:

- Snap beans
- Pole beans
- Leeks
- Parsnips
- Carrots

Gardening Tips and What to Have on Hand

Of course, growing crops in a drought is not only about picking the right plants. You also need to understand what to do to get them to thrive. Here are some things to do now, and some things to keep in mind for the future.

- Buy drought-resistant seeds now and start growing the crops. Some deep-root plants, like carrots and parsnips, do better once they are established. If you try to grow them during a serious drought, it may be a challenge if you haven't grown them before.
- Be vigilant about weeds. Weeds compete with the things you plant for water. You can keep more of your precious water for vegetables and fruits if you keep weeds away from your garden beds.
- Cover your entire garden with three or four inches of mulch. You can use almost any organic material for mulch, including grass clippings, leaves, or pine needles. Anything you use will protect the water in the soil by keeping it from evaporating. As the mulch breaks down, it will send nutrients into the soil, making it easier for plants to grow. A thick layer of mulch will also inhibit the spread of weeds.
- Use compost. Chemical fertilizers increase the amount of water plants need to grow, and they're not good for your family, either. Instead, compost your food scraps and use them to fertilize your garden.
- Collect rainwater. Rainwater is perfectly safe to use to water your crops, and you don't need to purify it first. Install rain barrels or other containers to catch whatever falls so you can use it as you need it.

- Group plants with similar watering needs together to make it easier to conserve water. You can put in a drip irrigation system if you want to, or just have separate beds so that you can control the amount of water you give to each type of plant.
- Use tubes and drip irrigation to give your garden a deep watering that will encourage plants to develop strong root systems. The deeper a plant's roots grow, the better able it will be to survive in a drought.
- Think about growing vegetables in pots. Pot gardening allows you a little more control over the amount of water you give plants, and it may be a good choice for vegetables that need wetter soil to grow.
- Think about ways to use water twice. For example, if you are taking a shower put a bucket or container in the tub to catch unused water. You can then use it to water your garden.
- If you have non-edible plants you want to water, you can save the water that you've used to rinse the dishes, or drain water from the washing machine after you have cleaned your clothes. Do not use that water on edible plants, though, because it will make them unsafe to eat.

One final note. Certain plants are water hogs and do not make good choices in a drought. Plants to avoid include:

- Broccoli
- Chickpeas
- Lentils
- Peas
- Asparagus

If you choose your crops wisely and do what you can to protect the soil, you can use your garden to provide healthy food for your family, even if you don't have water.

SANITATION WITHOUT WATER

One of the things that is the hardest for most American when they have limited water is dealing with sanitation. We are accustomed to using vast amounts of water every day to clean our bodies, our laundry, and our homes. This chapter will give you some practical advice on how to deal with sanitation when you don't have much water.

Cleaning Clothes

There are two basic methods of cleaning clothes. The first is for times when you have a little bit of water to use. In a serious drought, you probably won't be able to do this, but in a shortage you can collect extra water from the shower and use it to do your laundry. For this method you will need:

- A metal washtub
- A plunger
- A commercial salad spinner
- A clothes line
- A basket

To wash clothes, fill the bucket halfway with water, add soap, and use the plunger to dissolve the soap and make bubbles. Start with your whites and mildly dirty clothes, because you'll use the same water for everything. Save extremely dirty or stinky laundry, like socks, until the end.

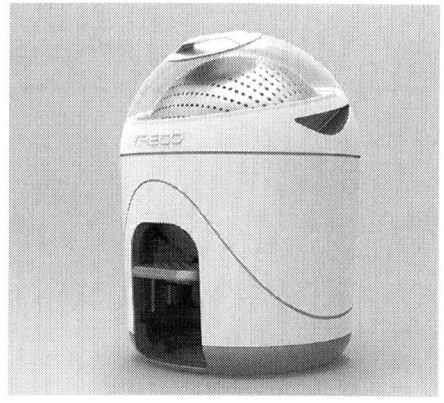

Pile the clothes into the bucket – don't do too many at once. Use the plunger as a manual agitator to force the soap through the clothes. You can use an old-fashioned washboard if something needs to be scrubbed. When they clothes are clean, put them into the basket of the salad spinner and pour water over them to rinse out as much of the soap as you can. Spin the clothes to remove excess water, and then put them in your laundry basket. When you're done, hang them on a clothesline to dry.

Note: drying clothes this way will take a while because the salad spinner will not remove as much water as the spin cycle of a washing machine would. Put the clothesline in direct sunlight for speedier drying.

To clean clothes without soap and water, use the sun as a natural cleaner and deodorizer. For best results, shake your clothes thoroughly to remove dust and debris. Then lay them out in direct sunlight. Don't lay them on the ground. Hang them on a clothesline, or drape them over a fence or bush. If you can, leave them out all day, turning them periodically. You can use this method to disinfect sleeping bags, too – just make sure to turn them inside out.

Personal Hygiene

Keeping your body clean can be tricky without water, but there are a few things you can do. First, lay in a supply of dry shampoo, and things like rubbing alcohol, hand sanitizer, baby wipes, and mouthwash. You can brush dry shampoo through your hair to keep it clean. You can use baby wipes to clean your body. You'll want to use them sparingly to conserve them, but at least you can clean your armpits and genitals to remove odors and kill bacteria.

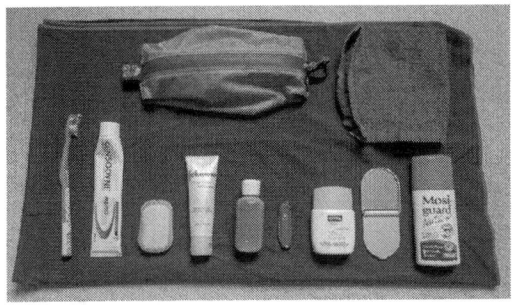

You can use rubbing alcohol to remove germs and bacteria, but it is very drying to be careful not to overdo it. Hand sanitizer can be slightly less drying and have the same effect. Finally, mouthwash actually makes a very good disinfectant. You can use it on your armpits instead of deodorant.

Disposing of Human Waste without Water

One of the most important things you need to know for any water emergency is what to do with human waste. The average person produces between 800 and 2,000 milliliters of urine every day, and about an ounce of feces per twelve pounds of body weight. That means that a person who weighs 160 pounds would produce approximately one pound of feces per day. That's a lot of waste material to cope with if there's no water, and few people know how to deal with safely.

Before we get into how to manage human waste safely, let's talk about what can happen if you don't. The earthquake that hit Haiti in 2010 knocked out power and water for the entire area. One of the reasons the aftermath of the earthquake was so deadly was because of the lack of sanitations. Diseases like cholera and typhoid spread rapidly and added to the death count. Similar situations have occurred after other natural disasters.

Here's what you can do to protect yourself. If you are hooked up to the municipal water supply, the first thing to do is to determine if the main sewer line is working. If it isn't, do NOT flush your toilet. Doing that could lead to a situation where the sewers back up into your toilets, sinks, and bathtubs.

If the main sewer is working, but the water is not flowing, you can flush your toilet by either putting water in the tank or pouring it directly into the bowl to trigger the siphon effect. You can continue to flush (as long as you have water) if you have a septic system. In a situation with very limited water, you have a couple of options. Let's look at what to do if you live in a suburban or rural area, and then at what you can do in the city.

Regardless of where you live, it is important not to leave human waste exposed. It will attract flies and other insects, and can quickly lead to the spread of disease as insects land first on waste, and then on food.

Suburban/Rural Area

In a suburban or rural area where you have access to the ground, you have two basic options. The first is to dig cat holes – small holes in the ground that act as makeshift latrines. To make one, simply dig a hole four to six inches in diameter, and six to eight inches deep. Do your business in the hole, throw your toilet paper or leaves in there too, and then cover it with the dirt you took out of the whole. If you use this method, keep a couple of things in mind:

- Keep all cat holes at least 200 feet from water sources.
- Do not dig cat holes in an area where water runs off or collects.
- Try to space out cat holes across a wide area.
- If possible, dig cat holes in areas that get direct sunlight to speed decomposition.

For a long-term water emergency, instead of cat holes you can dig a latrine – basically a trench that is intended for repeated use. At the minimum, you'll want it to be 1.5 feet wide, 2 feet deep, and 1 foot deep. You can lay planks over it so that people have a place to sit when they use it. You should also build a privacy partition. Since the latrine is intended for multiple uses, you will need to keep a supply of quicklime, wood ash, or dirt nearby and instruct everyone in your family to cover their waste after they use the latrine. Covering it will keep flies and other pests from landing on it and spreading disease.

Urban Area

Disposing of waste in urban areas is trickier, but not impossible. The same basic rules apply. Your primary concern needs to be keeping your living environment free of pests and disease. That means finding a way to collect, cover, and dispose of waste while keeping insects away from it.

If you want to continue using your toilet, get as much water out of the bowl as you can, and then line the bowl with doubled up heavy-duty trash bags. Have people use the toilet, and then sprinkle it with wood ash, quicklime, kitty litter or sawdust to keep the insects away. When the bowl is about two-thirds of the way full, remove it, sprinkle it generously with quicklime or whatever disinfectant you have available, tie it off, and place it in a sealed container to dispose of when you are able.

Another option if you don't want to use the toilet is to use a 5-gallon bucket. Follow the same basic procedure. Line the bucket with doubled up heavy-duty trash bags. You can buy toilet seats to fit a bucket, or just lay a couple of pieces of wood across the top for people to sit on. Follow the same rules as you would if you were using the toilet – everyone who uses it must sprinkle their waste with wood ash, quicklime, or something of that nature after every use. When it gets about two-thirds of the way full, tie it off and temporarily store it in a sealable container until you can get rid of it.

A couple of products are bags that are specially made to handle human waste. You can find them here. They're meant for people who are camping, but you can use them in an urban area if you want to. The same company makes toilet deodorant that promises to neutralize odors. You can find that here.

Finally, if you have money to spend, you might want to consider buying a composting toilet that will take human waste and turn it into usable compost.

The most important thing to remember is that you cannot allow waste to pile up without covering it or treating it. If you recall, a big part of the worst case scenario from earlier in the book had to do with the spread of disease and the subsequent increase in mortality rates. You cannot afford to take the disposal of waste lightly. If you are in the city and the people around you are not taking it seriously, you may need to take the time to educate them about proper procedures. Obviously, your family is your top priority, but diseases don't discriminate. Even if you take care of your own waste properly, if you live in an apartment building or condo surrounded by people who are mismanaging their waste, you will be at risk for infection and disease too. This is one area where sharing your knowledge is important – it could even save your life

DO IT YOURSELF

Not everybody has the money to spend thousands of dollars buying solar stills and water filters. The purpose of this chapter is to give you simple, step-by-step instructions to make what you need to ensure you have clean, safe water for your family to drink.

Water Filters

Let's start with water filters. Removing sediment and toxins from water is important. A filter will not completely ensure safe water – you'll need to boil it for that – but filtering water is an important first step. Since you already have instructions on how to filter water using charcoal, this section will focus on a couple of different methods you can use to make a filter using a plastic bottle or a jar. Most of the components are things you already have around your house.

Cloth Filter

The simplest form of filter is a cloth filter. To make one, simply place a clean bandanna or another square of fabric over the mouth of a jar and secure it with rubber bands, twine, or whatever else you have handy. Pour the water over the cloth. Large items like sediment, insects, and other organic material will be caught on the cloth. You should still boil the water you filter, but the filtering will remove a lot of troublesome things from the water, making it taste and look better.

Multi-layer Filter

Some of the most effective filters use multiple layers to help remove different-sized particles. To make a simple one, drill a hole in the cap of a 2-liter bottle. Saw the large end of the bottle, and then layer in the following items:

- Stuff coffee filters or gauze into the neck of the bottle.
- Next, layer in crushed charcoal.
- Put a layer of sand on top of the charcoal.
- Put a layer of gravel on top of the sand.
- Repeat the last two layers, ending with gravel on top.
- Pour the water through. It should trickle down through the layers and come out significantly cleaner on the other end.

Another method, if you don't have charcoal, is to use pillow stuffing at the bottom of the bottle, then top with a layer of sand and a layer of rocks.

Note: Very dirty water may need to be filtered more than once, and you still need to boil it to purify it after it's been filtered.

Atmospheric Water Generator

As you saw earlier in the book, most commercial atmospheric stills are very expensive. Here is a simple method you can use to make one for only a little over three hundred dollars.

What You Need
1 new dehumidifier (around $200.00)

1 water filter system (hardware or home shops, around $125)
1 32" piece of clear vinyl tubing (pet supply or aquarium store, $3)
1 Servo Voltage Regulator (in case of power fluctuations) $75
2 4" X 9" 3M scrubber pads, $2
1 zip tie, $0.10

Tools
¾" drill with a ½" drill bit
Phillips-head screwdriver
Scissors

Instructions
1) Remove all covers from the humidifier and rinse the inside using a garden hose. (Do not use high pressure, which will damage the condenser flanges.) Dry thoroughly.
2) Remove the knockout for the hose on the back cover of the humidifier.
3) Run the clear vinyl tube through the knockout and attach it to the hose connector (you are bypassing the internal reservoir).
4) Cut the scrubber pads to fit the air filter holder on the front of the

machine and attach the filter holder to the front panel.
5) Wash the water filter unit and filter before using it.

6) Drill a hole in the top of the filter unit. Run the vinyl tubing from the dehumidifier through the hole and into the filter. Do not crimp the house. Place the lid on top of the filter.
7) Plug the filter unit into the servo regulator.

Turn on the machine, and let it run for six to eight hours depending on the level of humidity in the air. When the upper filter area is full, let the water filter into the lower storage area. The water should come out neutral with a 6.0 pH level, and after it filters it should be at about 7.4 or 8.0, depending on the type of filter you use.

Desalinator

Here are two methods to make a desalinator. The first is very inexpensive and easy, but will only collect a little bit of water. The second will cost more to make, but it will also yield more water.

Method 1

What You Need:

Two bowls, one large and one small

Plastic wrap

Rubber band or string

A rock or weight

1. Fill a large bowl about halfway with salt water.
2. Place a smaller glass bowl inside of it.
3. Cover the bowl with plastic, making sure to leave enough that the plastic sags in the middle a bit. Secure the plastic with a rubber band or string.

4. Place the bowl in the sun, and weight the plastic in the middle with a rock.

The heat from the sun will cause the water to evaporate and rise up as steam. The plastic will trap the steam and cause it to condense and drip into the smaller bowl. After several hours, you can remove the smaller bowl, which will contain desalinated, drinkable water. Make sure to dispose of the other water carefully. It will be very salty, and could be harmful to pets or plants.

Method 2

What You Need:

- A stove or fire
- 2 pots
- 1 water catchment container
- Aluminum foil
- Plastic tubing, 2 lengths
- Wet cloth

1. Take a square of aluminum foil. Wrap one corner of it tightly around one end of the tubing, and form the rest of it into a funnel shape. This will be used to trap the steam.
2. Fill one pot with salt water and secure the aluminum foil over the top. Make sure the tubing does not touch the surface of the water.
3. Place a second pot of cool water nearby, but at a slightly higher level than the first pot. Let the middle of the tube dip into the cool water, this will help the steam to condense.
4. Place your catchment container below the second pot, and put the other end of the tube into the container.
5. To keep the plastic tubing cool, wrap it with a water-soaked cloth if necessary. If you are using salt water to wet the

cloth, make sure that the salt water cannot drip into your catchment container.
6. Bring the water to a boil. As the steam condenses, the water level in the tube will rise and drip into your catchment container.

If you feel it would help to see a video of this device in action, you can find one here. It is important to note here that this is not the most energy-efficient way of collecting water, but in an emergency it could save your life.

Solar Still

What You Need:
- ¾" plywood
- 1 sheet of glass, 24" long
- 2 large (10" x 15") Pyrex dishes
- PEX drain
- Caulk

1. Build a plywood box large enough to hold the two Pyrex dishes. Use a double width of plywood to prevent warping. Make the back end of the box about three inches taller than the front.
2. Make a drop-down door for the back of the box that will allow you to remove the dishes.
3. Put hinges on the door, and seal it with weather stripping to make it airtight.
4. Use contact cement to glue reflective foil to the inside of the door.
5. Paint the inside of the box black to help capture heat.
6. Drill a hole in the front of the box for the PEX drain. The whole should be about ½" from the top of the box.
7. Cut a 19" length of PEX and then cut it in half with a utility knife.

8. Drill three 1/8" holes in the PEX, insert it through the whole, and drill it to the side of the box.
9. Cut the sheet of glass to fit the top of the box and use caulk to attach it. Tape it down with painter's tape and let it sit overnight.

Once the still is built, fill the Pyrex dishes with water and close the back door. Place a catchment container underneath the PEX and set the still in the sun. The heat from the sun will cause the water in the dishes to evaporate and condense on the glass. It will run down through the PEX and into your catchment container.

For a complete video of how to build this still, including templates for the box, you can click here.

Vegetation Still

Here are two simple methods to make a vegetation still.

Method 1
- What You Need:
- Plastic bags
- Cord or twine
- Rocks

1. Find a non-toxic tree or plant.
2. Put a plastic bag over a branch fitting as many leaves into the bag as possible.
3. Place a rock in the bag to weight it and pull the bottom of the bag into a V shape.
4. Tie the bag securely with twine.

As the bag sits in the sun, the heat will cause water to evaporate from the leaves and condense on the inside of the bag. The rock will ensure that the water collects in the bottom of the bag. For best results, let the bag sit all day and collect it after it cools down at night for maximum condensation. You can have several of these makeshift stills working at once. After you collect the water, you can move the bags to a different area so they can start collecting water again.

Method 2

What You Need:

- Leaves
- Plastic wrap
- Tin cup
- Plastic tubing (optional)
- Rock

1. Dig a hole about 19" deep. Make sure to dig down until the soil starts to feel moist. Do not dig in the shade if you can avoid it.
2. Fill the hole with leaves and vegetation, place your cup in the middle of it, and cover it with plastic wrap. Seal the plastic by pouring sand or dirt around the edges.
3. If you have a plastic tube, put one end inside the cup before you seal the hole.
4. Place the rock on the plastic over the cup (make sure the plastic doesn't touch the cup or the water won't drip into it.)

As the sun heats up the earth and vegetation under the plastic, water will condense and run down the plastic into the cup. If you have a tube, you can use it to sip water from the cup without having to disturb the still.

When you have drawn all the moisture you can from the ground, you can dig a hole in a new spot or simply dig deeper in the same spot. You will also need to add more vegetation.

The good thing about most of these water collection devices is that they are inexpensive to make, and most of them can be used more than once. If you have stored water, it may make sense to save it and use whatever water you can collect from the air and land before dipping into your stored water. In the event of a long-term drought, vegetation and soil may dry up to the point where you can no longer collect water from them. If you have reason to believe that will happen, then save your stored water and get what you can elsewhere.

If you live near the ocean, it may make sense to collect salt water right away and start the desalination process. Anything you can do to make your stored water last longer is a good thing.

WATER SURVIVAL PLAN AND CHECKLIST

It should be clear by now why it is so important to be prepared for a water crisis. Human beings can only live a few days without water, and if there is a serious drought or other emergency, people who have stored water and prepared will be the ones who survive.

To make things easier for you, here are some checklists you can use to make sure you have what you need.

Water Storage:

- Food-grade plastic bottles
- Food-grade plastic barrels
- Dish soap
- Unscented chlorine bleach
- Gloves
- Sharpie (for dating bottles)

A good rule of thumb is to store one gallon of water per day for each person and pet in your household.

Emergency Water Sources

It may be helpful to have a checklist of places where you can get water in an emergency:

- Melted ice cubes
- Liquids in canned foods
- Water heater
- Pipes
- Toilet tanks (not bowls)
- Swimming pool/hot tubs
- Gutters
- Fire hydrants
- Natural water (lakes, ponds, rivers, streams, brooks, springs)
- Man-made sources (fountains, water hazards on golf courses, reservoirs)

If you are unsure about the purity of any water you collect, filter and boil it before drinking it.

Water Testing Supplies

If you want to be able to test water, you should have a testing kit on hand:

First Alert Drinking Water Test Kit

PurTest Home Water Analysis Testing Kit

Water Purifying Supplies
- Unscented chlorine bleach
- Chlorine dioxide tablets
- Iodine drops or tablets
- Filters

Water Harvesting Supplies and Devices

Devices:
- Solar still
- Desalinator
- Vegetation still
- Atmospheric still

Supplies:
- Plywood
- Plastic tubing
- Glass
- Nails
- Screws

- Caulk
- Black paint
- PEX
- Glass or Pyrex dishes
- Plastic bags
- Cord or twine
- Pots
- Heat source (camp stove, etc.)
- Catchment containers
- Aluminum foil

Other items

Here are some other items to have on hand:

- Heavy duty trash bags
- Toilet deodorizer
- 5-gallon buckets
- Activated charcoal
- Quicklime
- Sawdust
- Kitty litter
- Industrial salad spinner
- Clothesline
- Metal tub for laundry
- Clean toilet plunger
- Google Maps printouts of water in your area

Groceries:
- Canned fruits
- Canned vegetables

- Canned meats
- Bottled water
- Bottled juice and other beverages
- Seeds for foods that grow with little water:
    o Amaranth
    o Corn
    o Sweet potatoes
    o Watermelon
    o Black-eyed peas
    o Nopale cactus
    o Jerusalem artichokes
    o Leeks
    o Parsnips
    o Carrots
    o Pole beans
    o Lima beans

Non-perishable foods
- Granola bars
- Trail mix
- Jerky
- Shelf-stable milk
- Nuts
- Seeds
- Dried fruits
- Pasta
- Dried beans and peas
- MREs

Personal hygiene items:

- Hand sanitizer
- Rubbing alcohol
- Dry shampoo

- Mouthwash
- Laundry detergent

CONCLUSION

Thank you for reading Water Crisis Survival Guide.

The information in this book is meant to help you prepare for the coming water crisis. Sometimes prepping is about getting ready for something that might seem improbable, but in this case, the crisis is inevitable. The signs are visible everywhere, in California, Ohio, Detroit, and the Pacific Northwest. The United States and Mexico are already at odds about the water in the Rio Grande as Texas is experiencing record droughts.

The situation would be dire enough if all we had to worry about were a severe drought, but there are other issues to consider as well. The United States is vulnerable to attack by terrorists and hostile nations, and our water supply does not have adequate protection. If

ISIS or Al Qaeda wanted to cripple the country and kill millions of people, all they would need to do would be to introduce chemical or biological agents into our water supply. The entire country would be thrown into chaos.

Storing potable water is an important first step, and that's where you should start. Begin by calculating how much water your family needs per day, and then decide how much you want to store. The minimum amount you need to have on hand is two weeks of potable water. For a family of four with a pet dog, that would amount to 70 gallons of water.

As mentioned earlier in the book, your best bet is to store water in more than one way. If you have the space to keep them, you may want to invest in some 55-gallon barrels made of food-grade plastic. They will take up lace space than individual bottles. However, because they're not portable, you should also store some water in smaller bottles. You can buy bottled water, use sterilized soda or juice bottles, or buy some of the 5-gallon jugs used by campers. Portability is essential if you want to be able to bug out.

Once you have an emergency water supply, your next step should be laying in the supplies you need to gather and purify additional water. Print out Google Maps of your area, build or buy a still, and gather essential things like plastic bags, water purification tablets, bleach, and iodine drops. Use the checklists in the book as a guideline.

You also need to make preparations for hygiene and sanitation. Remember, in a serious shortage where the municipal water supply is unavailable, sanitation is going to deteriorate quickly. You need to have supplies on hand so that you can keep things safe for your family. The items you need are on the checklists in the last chapter.

Finally, it is important to give some thought to long-term survival. The water shortage may end up being the thing that precipitates a wide-scale crisis. In the event of a mega drought or catastrophic attack on our water supplies, it would not take long for things to become dangerous, both in terms of hygiene and civil unrest. If you follow the advice in this book, you will be better prepared to handle what happens than 99% of the people around you, and that means you need to be prepared to defend what you have. In certain cases, such as sanitation protocol, it may make sense to share your knowledge about how to cope with waste. If you live in close quarters with other people and don't have a place to bug out to, a neighbor's lack of sanitation can have a direct impact on your family's health and safety. Keep that in mind.

However, sharing information about sanitation does not mean that you should feel any obligation to share your water. This is about survival. When the crisis hits, do whatever you can to hold on to your stockpile of water. If you can collect water from other places, do it. You're going to be in competition with other people for the resources that are available. You don't have to let on that you have a supply of water laid in – in fact, it is better not to do so, especially if there are people watching what you do. There's no need to make yourself a target if you don't have to.

The best way to protect your family is to keep your stored water out of sight. The best place to store water is in a cool, dry place such as a cellar. Even if you have 55-gallon barrels, don't leave them outside. Put them in a place where they won't be seen from the road. The less information your neighbors have about what you have on hand, the better.

The water crisis is coming. There is nothing any of us can do to prevent it, but you can take action now to make sure that your family members and pets have the water they need to survive. Most people are not going to be prepared when the critical moment arrives. They will be panicked, scrambling to get their hands on bottled water and purification supplies. The point of doing your prep now is that you won't have any need to panic. You can stay calm, knowing that your family is safe.